Copyright ©2020 ARNOLD KUNTZ PH.D

All rights reserved. No part of this publication may be reproduced, distributed, or transmitted in any form or by any means, including photocopying, recording, or other electronic or mechanical methods, without the prior written permission of the publisher, except in the case of brief quotations embodied in critical reviews and certain other noncommercial uses permitted by copyright law.

CONTENTS

INTRODUCTION

Pharmacodynamics: Cannabis and Cannabinoids Act on Multiple Pain Targets

    The history of cannabis: Weed and pain control

    Key Findings about Cannabis for Pain Management

    What is the best marijuana for treating pain?

        Whole plant or THC only? The entourage effect

    Cannabis sativa and the entourage effect

    How CBD and THC influence the user experience together

    Benefits of high-CBD strains for treating pain

    Benefits of high-THC strains for treating pain

    Anecdotal evidence

    High THC or high CBD for pain?

    Best cannabis strains for pain

    Does CBD oil work for chronic pain management?

    Effects of CBD

    Does CBD make you high?

What is CBD oil?

    Benefits and pain relief

        Other uses

    Dosage

    CBD oil for back pain

- CBD lotion for pain
- Dosage amounts of cannabis and CBD for pain
- Cannabis sativa is good for pain
- Side effects
  - Other considerations
- How long does cbd oil take to work
- How Much CBD Should I Take?
- How Long CBD Takes to Enter Your Bloodstream
  - Factor 1: Method of Intake
  - Factor 2: Dosage & Potency
  - Factor 3: CBD Quality
  - Factor 4: Individual Biology
  - Factor 5: Consistency
- Body Weight
- Metabolism
- Endocannabinoid Balance
- Feeling out How CBD Works for You
- What Kind of CBD Should I Take?
- What Time of Day Should I Take It?
- How Often Should I Take CBD?
- How Long Does It Take for CBD to Work?

CONCLUSION

INTRODUCTION

Pain is one of the most common symptoms of disease. Acute pain is usually successfully managed with non-steroidal anti-inflammatory drugs (NSAIDs) and/or opioids, but chronic pain is often difficult to treat and can be very disabling. An adjuvant is a drug that is not primarily intended to be an analgesic but can be used to reduce pain either alone or in combination with other pain medications. Some of these drugs have been known for some time, but their acceptance has waxed and waned over time. However, new approaches to targeting the pain pathway have been developed and adjuvant analgesics continue to attract both scientific and medical interest as constituents' of a multimodal approach to pain management. The role of cannabis plant and its components, called cannabinoids, as adjuvant analgesics in the treatment of chronic pain, has been the subject of longstanding controversy.

Flowering plants within the genus Cannabis (also known as marijuana) in the family Cannabaceae have been cultivated for thousands of years in many parts of the world for spiritual, recreational and medicinal purposes. Preparations of the cannabis plant, which are taken by smoking or oral ingestion, have been observed to produce analgesic, anti-anxiety, anti-spasmodic, muscle relaxant, anti-inflammatory and anticonvulsant effects. However, the prohibition of cannabis cultivation, supply and possession from the middle of the 20th century (due to its psychoactivity and potential for producing dependence), has impeded cannabis research. In recent years there is a growing debate about cannabis use for medical purposes. In many countries cannabis use for medical reasons is legal and some countries have also decriminalized or legalized the recreational use of cannabis.

The term medical cannabis is used to refer to the physician-recommended use of cannabis and its constituents, cannabinoids, to treat disease or improve symptoms. The use of cannabis and cannabinoids may be limited by its psychotropic side effects (e.g., euphoria, anxiety, paranoia) or other central nervous system (CNS)-related undesired effects (cognitive impairment, depression of motor activity, addiction), which occur because of activation of cannabinoid CB1 receptors in the CNS . As interest in the use of cannabinoids as adjunctive therapy for pain management has increased in the last decades, there has been a continuing need for an increase in cannabis research and bridging the knowledge gap about cannabis and its use in pain treatment. Therefore, research on cannabis and cannabinoids has increased dramatically in recent years. However, there are several obstacles that need to be overcome, such as the regulations and policies that restrict access to the cannabis products, funding limitations, and numerous methodological challenges (drug delivery, the placebo issue, etc.).

PHARMACODYNAMICS: CANNABIS AND CANNABINOIDS ACT ON MULTIPLE PAIN TARGETS

For many years it was assumed that the chemical components of the cannabis plant, cannabinoids, produce analgesia by activating specific receptors throughout the body, in particular CB1, which are found predominantly in the CNS, and CB2, found predominantly in cells involved with immune function. However, recently this picture has become much more complicated, as it has been recognized that cannabinoids, both plant-derived and endogenous, act simultaneously on multiple pain targets within the peripheral and CNS. Beside acting on cannabinoid CB1/CB2 receptors, they may reduce pain through interaction with the putative non-CB1/CB2 cannabinoid G protein-coupled receptor (GPCR) 55 or GPCR 18 (GPR18), also known as the N-arachidonoyl glycine, and other well-known GPCRs, such as the opioid or serotonin (5-HT) receptors. In addition, many studies have reported the ability of certain cannabinoids to modulate nuclear receptors (peroxisome proliferator-activated receptors (PPARs), cys loop ligand-gated ion channels or transient receptor potential (TRP) channels (TRPV, TRPA, and TRPM subfamilies), among others. It has been shown that all these receptors represent potentially attractive targets for the therapeutic use of cannabinoids in the treatment of pain. Moreover, TRPV1 and CB1 or CB2 are colocalized at peripheral and/or central neurons (sensory neurons, dorsal root ganglia, spinal cord, brain neurons), which results in their intracellular crosstalk in situations where these receptors are involved simultaneously. New data also demonstrate a variety of interactions between cannabinoid, opioid, and TRPV1 receptors in pain modulation. All of these provide an opportunity for the development of new multiple target ligands and polypharmacological drugs with improved efficacy and devoid of side effects for the treatment of pain.

Several lines of evidence indicate that cannabinoids may contribute to pain relief through an anti-inflammatory action. In addition, non-cannabinoid constituents of the cannabis plant that belong to miscellaneous groups of natural products (terpenoids and flavonoids) may contribute to the analgesic, as well as the anti-inflammatory effects of cannabis.

THE HISTORY OF CANNABIS: WEED AND PAIN CONTROL

Throughout history, cannabis has been cultivated and used for its medicinal purposes. Evidence suggests that it was cultivated by humans as far back as 12,000 years ago. Throughout this time, the cannabis plant has been exalted as miraculous and cursed as a danger to the fabric of society. Yet, throughout this varied past, one thing has remained the same: Cannabis has been used as a plant medicine for the treatment of an impressively wide array of diseases. The earliest evidence of its medicinal use dates back to 2700 BC when Chinese Emperor Shen Nung documented the analgesic (pain-relieving) properties. Shen Nung is considered by many to be the father of Chinese medicine, which has helped to heal people through the use of natural remedies for thousands of years. We have now entered a time where the benefits of this plant are beginning to come back to the forefront of the discussion. Indeed, countless individuals across the world have access to legal marijuana for chronic pain conditions.

KEY FINDINGS ABOUT CANNABIS FOR PAIN MANAGEMENT

Cannabinoids and cannabis are old drugs but now they are a promising new therapeutic strategy for pain treatment.

Cannabinoids (plant-derived, synthetic) themselves or endocannabinoid-directed therapeutic strategies have been shown to be effective in different animal models of pain (acute nociceptive, neuropathic, inflammatory). However, medical cannabis is not equally effective against all types of pain in humans.

A recent meta-analysis of clinical trials of medical cannabis for chronic pain found substantial evidence encouraging its use in pharmacotherapy of chronic pain. Also, it was shown that medical cannabis may only moderately reduce chronic pain, similar all other currently available analgesic drugs. However, controlled comparative studies on the efficacy and safety of cannabis/cannabinoids and other analgesics, including opioids, are missing. Inhaled (smoked or vaporized) cannabis is constantly effective in reducing neuropathic pain and this effect is dose-related and can be achieved with a concentration of cannabis THC lower than 10%. Compared to oral cannabinoids, the effect of inhaled cannabis is more rapid, predictable and can be titrated. Compared to inhaled cannabis, the effectiveness of oral cannabinoids in reducing the sensory component of neuropathic pain seems to be less convincing and oral cannabinoids in general may be less tolerable. However, data suggest that they may improve secondary measures such as sleep, quality of life and patient satisfaction.

There are no controlled clinical trials on the use of inhaled cannabis for the treatment of cancer or rheumatic (osteoarthritis, rheumatoid arthritis, and fibromyalgia) pain. Whether oral cannabinoids reduce the intensity of chronic cancer pain is not completely clear. Recent long-term studies of nabiximols are not encouraging. Studies shows that oral cannabinoids have inadequate efficacy in rheumatological pain conditions. Also, oral cannabinoids do not reduce acute postoperative or chronic abdominal pain. In general, the efficacy of medical cannabis in pain treatment is not completely clear due to several limitations. Clinical trials are scarce and most were of short duration, with relatively small sample sizes, heterogeneous patient populations, different types of cannabinoids, a range of dosages, variability in the assessment of domains of pain (sensory, affective) and modest effect sizes. Therefore, further larger studies examining specific cannabinoids and strains of cannabis, using improved and objective pain measurements, appropriate dosages and duration of treatment in homogeneous patient populations need to be carried out.

The current review of evidence from clinical trials of

medicinal cannabis suggests that the adverse effects of its short-term use are modest, most of them are not serious and are self-limiting. Long-term safety assessment of medicinal cannabis is based on scant clinical trials, so the evidence is limited, and the safety interpretation should be taken cautiously. More research is needed to evaluate the adverse effects of long-term use of medical cannabis. In view of the limited effect size and the low but not unimportant risk of serious, adverse events, a more precise determination of the risk-to-benefit ratio for medicinal cannabis in pain treatment is needed to help establishing evidence-based policy implementation. Current evidence supports the use of medical cannabis in the treatment of chronic pain in adults. Monitoring and follow-up of patients is obligatory.

WHAT IS THE BEST MARIJUANA FOR TREATING PAIN?

Should patients turn to singular compounds found in the plant, or turn to the plant itself? If using the whole plant, what marijuana strains are the best for providing relief from pain?

Whole plant or THC only? The entourage effect

When you compare Western medicine to traditional medicine the world over, one of the most striking differences is the need in the West to pinpoint one specific molecule that is responsible for treating a disease or symptom. This viewpoint stands contrary to the idea of holistic medicine, where you take something in its entirety for medicinal purposes. The 'entourage effect' is a new term coined to describe the idea that all compounds found in the cannabis plant work synergistically, providing more benefit together than the individual compounds would provide alone.

CANNABIS SATIVA AND THE ENTOURAGE EFFECT

The Cannabis sativa plant is one of the greatest present-day examples of this tug-of-war between Western medicine and traditional medicine. If you live in a state where marijuana is legal, you may have noticed products being advertised as "isolates" or "whole plant extracts." Proponents of the isolationist Western medicine theories would advocate for isolates, which are simply products containing just tetrahydrocannabinol (THC) or just cannabidiol (CBD), or far less commonly, any of the other individual phytocannabinoids.

THC is the psychotropic phytocannabinoid that is to thank for the "high" effect users get when they smoke weed. It has been found to have a variety of health-related benefits for the user. CBD is the second most well-known cannabinoid found in cannabis, and like most of the other phytocannabinoids, it is non-psychotropic. These are the two most abundant and well-studied cannabinoids in marijuana, and both have been found in numerous published studies to have pain-relieving properties in humans. While they may be the most abundant, THC and CBD are certainly not the only compounds found in cannabis that are known to exert positive effects on human health. In every cannabis plant, there is a unique mixture of hundreds of plant compounds, comprised of phytocannabinoids, terpenes, and flavonoids. Research suggests that these compounds too have an influence on our neurochemistry, and together they may work synergistically, producing better improvements in pain relief than anyone would produce on its own. This research supports the idea that it is best to use the whole cannabis plant, with CBD, THC, and the natural medley of additional compounds. This harmony between the various plants chemicals found in marijuana is colloquially referred to as the entourage effect.

HOW CBD AND THC INFLUENCE THE USER EXPERIENCE TOGETHER

The most well-studied compounds found in the marijuana plant that support the idea of the entourage effect are THC and CBD, which have been found to work differently together than when separate. Using these two compounds in concert has been shown to help mitigate side effects and enhance efficacy, with CBD plus THC showing more benefit for some conditions than THC alone. Studies have confirmed that CBD helps to counteract some of the sedative, "high" feeling, anxiety, and rapid heartbeat that is associated with THC consumption. It has also been found to extend the half-life of THC, which may help to extend the pain-relieving benefits. This has allowed the use of higher doses of THC in clinical trials for the treatment of pain caused by multiple sclerosis, peripheral neuropathic pain, intractable cancer pain, and rheumatoid arthritis. When used in concert, a greater efficacy in treating these types of pain have been observed. You may be wondering, what is the ideal balance, or ratio, of CBD to THC? Every strain of bud that you can purchase at a dispensary will be labeled with its THC and CBD content, which can be helpful when choosing which strain to choose for pain relief.

BENEFITS OF HIGH-CBD STRAINS FOR TREATING PAIN

CBD has been found to exhibit enhancements in treating pain both when used on its own and when used in combination with THC. When used alone, CBD is largely best for inflammatory pain, such as that caused by arthritis or injuries. In one animal study on arthritis pain, it was found that the topical application of CBD led to a reduction in inflammation and pain. Another animal study found that CBD helps to reduce neuropathic pain through the suppression of chronic inflammation. CBD does not directly bind to the receptors found in the endocannabinoid system but rather works to modulate the effects of the endocannabinoids (the cannabinoids found naturally in our bodies) as well as working as a CB1 receptor antagonist. The main mechanism by which CBD is thought to help mediate pain is by reducing inflammation, largely by blocking inflammatory mediators. It is also believed to potentiate glycine receptors, which help to regulate pain at the spinal level. This suppresses both neuropathic and inflammatory pain.

BENEFITS OF HIGH-THC STRAINS FOR TREATING PAIN

THC is used clinically for the treatment of pain and studies find it helps relieve central and neuropathic pain. It is also used to help reduce pain in cancer, AIDS, and fibromyalgia patients, for which resistance to other pain treatments have been found. The mode of action for THC is as a partial CB1 receptor agonist, which means that it will bind to these receptors but not fully which leads to the variability in effects documented when THC is present with other CB1 agonists, antagonists or both. It has been found to impact the serotonergic, dopaminergic, and glutamatergic systems an action which may contribute to its pain-relieving benefits. Additionally, THC has been found to act as an anti-inflammatory agent.

ANECDOTAL EVIDENCE

While human studies have found benefits from the use of THC, CBD, and whole-plant marijuana in relieving pain, much of the evidence for this use comes from user reports and surveys. In a survey of those suffering from chronic, non-cancer pain in Canada it was found that 35% of respondents reported using cannabis for pain relief. Another study found that, out of nearly 3,000 patients using medical cannabis, 97% reported that they were able to decrease their use of opioids when also using medical marijuana, with most reporting that the relief they experienced with cannabis was on par with other pain medications.

HIGH THC OR HIGH CBD FOR PAIN?

When searching for the best cannabis strains for pain relief, you will first want to consider how much THC and CBD is found in the strain. Generally, you will find the most relief from a strain that has large quantities of both CBD and THC, and a high CBD: THC ratio. This is because CBD can help to mediate the side effects of THC while also providing additional anti-inflammatory and analgesic properties.

There are certain times where you may prefer the effects of a higher THC or higher CBD strain. One example would be if you are experiencing inflammation, yet you are wanting to go about your day normally, without the psychotropic effects of THC. In this situation, a high-CBD low-THC strain can provide relief without much of an impact on mental function. Other times you may be in enough pain that you would like something that takes your mind off the pain while also offering pain relief. In this situation, the greater "high" that you would experience with a high-THC strain could be of benefit.

BEST CANNABIS STRAINS FOR PAIN

There are a few things that you will want to consider outside of simple percentage CBD and THC. One of these considerations is the 'type' of cannabis you are purchasing. There are three categories that your medical marijuana can fall into:

- Indica
- Sativa
- Hybrid (a mixture of both indica and sativa)

While this is not an exact science, users tend to report more effective pain-relieving properties with indicas. In one survey, participants reported that indicas helped more than sativas when it came to headaches, joint pain, neuropathy, and spasticity. Users also reported indicas to be more helpful when it comes to sleep and sedation. Lastly, there are countless user reports on specific strains of weed that have been found to be powerful for relieving pain. While some of these strains are high CBD, indica strains, some strains of weed used for pain do not fall into this category. It may be that the other cannabinoids, terpenes, and flavonoids have come together in a harmonious balance that leads to strong pain-relieving properties.

DOES CBD OIL WORK FOR CHRONIC PAIN MANAGEMENT?

Many people use cannabidiol (CBD) to relieve pain. Understanding CBD can help overcome the stigma associated with it. CBD oil is derived from the cannabis plant. People report using this oil for relief from pain, anxiety, depression, and sleep disorders.

There is limited evidence from human studies to support the benefits of CBD oil, due to restrictions on the use of and research on cannabis. As cannabis is becoming legalized in various regions, research is gaining momentum and shows some promising results.

EFFECTS OF CBD

CBD is one of more than 100 compounds found in cannabis, called cannabinoids. Many plants contain cannabinoids, but people most commonly link these compounds to cannabis. Unlike other cannabinoids such as tetrahydrocannabinol (THC) CBD does not produce a euphoric "high." This is because CBD does not affect the same receptors as THC. The human body has an endocannabinoid system (ECS) that receives and translates signals from cannabinoids. It produces some cannabinoids of its own, which are called endocannabinoids. The ECS helps regulate functions such as sleep, immune-system responses, and pain. When THC enters the body, it produces a "high" feeling by affecting the brain's endocannabinoid receptors. This activates the brain's reward system, producing pleasure chemicals such as dopamine.

DOES CBD MAKE YOU HIGH?

CBD is an entirely different compound from THC, and its effects are very complex. It does not produce a "high" and does not impair a person's functioning, but it influences the body to use its own endocannabinoids more effectively. CBD influences many other receptor systems in our body and will influence the ECS in combination with other cannabinoids. For example, CBD can increase the body's levels of anandamide, a compound associated with regulating pain, which can reduce pain perception and improve mood. Cannabidiol may also limit inflammation in the brain and nervous system, which may benefit people experiencing pain, insomnia, and certain immune system responses.

WHAT IS CBD OIL?

Different varieties of cannabis plants such as hemp and marijuana contain different levels of chemical compounds.

How people breed the plant affects the CBD levels. Most CBD oil comes from industrial hemp, which usually has a higher CBD content than marijuana. Makers of CBD oil use different methods to extract the compound. The extract is then added to a carrier oil and called CBD oil. CBD oil comes in many different strengths, and people use it in various ways. It is best to discuss CBD oil with a doctor before using it.

BENEFITS AND PAIN RELIEF

Some evidence suggests that cannabis or CBD could have modest benefits for chronic pain. While CBD is a promising option for pain relief, research has not yet proven it safe and effective, and the Food and Drug Administration (FDA) have not approved CBD for treating pain. CBD could have benefits for relieving chronic pain, improving sleep, and reducing inflammation, but that these effects are condition-specific. More evidence is needed to determine the therapeutic potential of CBD and to determine safe and effective dosages for pain.

Here are some possible benefits of CBD oil:
Neuropathic pain
Neuropathic pain is pain caused by damage to the nerves. This type of pain is common in diseases such as multiple sclerosis, injuries such as herniated discs, and infections such as shingles. A review found that CBD helped with chronic neuropathy pain in humans. The research looked at 11 randomized controlled trials with 1,219 patients. However, it is concluded that the potential benefits of cannabis-based medicine might be outweighed by its potential harms.

Arthritis pain

A study used an animal model to see if CBD could help people with arthritis manage their pain. Research applied a topical gel containing CBD to rats with arthritis for 4 days. A significant drop in inflammation and signs of pain was noted, without additional side effects. People using CBD oil for arthritis may find relief from their pain, but more human studies need to be done to confirm these findings.

Multiple sclerosis
Multiple sclerosis (MS) is an autoimmune condition that affects the entire body through the nerves and brain. Muscle spasms are one of the most common symptoms of MS. These spasms can be so strong they cause constant pain in some people.

Short-term use of CBD oil could reduce the levels of muscle spasms a person feels. The results are modest, but many people reported a reduction in symptoms. More studies on humans are needed to verify these results.

Chronic pain
Research concluded that there is substantial evidence that cannabis is an effective treatment for chronic pain in adults. A separate study suggests that using CBD can reduce pain and inflammation. The researchers also found that subjects were not likely to build up a tolerance to the effects of CBD, so they would not need to increase their dose over time. They noted that cannabinoids, such as CBD, could offer helpful new treatments for people with chronic pain.

OTHER USES

CBD currently has a range of applications and promising possibilities.

These include:
Helping people quit smoking

Managing drug withdrawal

Treating seizures and epilepsy

Treating anxiety

Reducing some effects of Alzheimer's disease

Reducing antipsychotic effects for people with schizophrenia

Potentially combating type 1 diabetes and cancer in the future

Although more research is required to confirm the benefits of CBD oil, it is shaping up as a potentially promising and versatile treatment. The Food and Drug Administration (FDA) have approved one form of CBD, called Epidiolex, to treat two rare forms of epilepsy and to treat seizures caused by a rare condition called tuberous sclerosis complex. More generally, marijuana-derived CBD products are not yet legal at the federal level but are legal under the laws of some states. People should check their state's laws and those of any place they intend to travel.

They must keep in mind that the FDA do not approve or regulate nonprescription CBD products. As a result, labeling may be inaccurate.

DOSAGE

The FDA does not regulate CBD for most conditions. As a result, dosages are currently open to interpretation, and people should treat them with caution. Anyone who wishes to use CBD should first speak to a doctor about whether it will be beneficial or safe, and how much to take. The FDA has approved a purified form of CBD for some types of epilepsy, with the brand name Epidiolex. People using this medication should follow the doctor's advice about doses..

CBD OIL FOR BACK PAIN

Back pain is one of the most common forms of both acute and chronic pain. Acute back pain tends to be caused by an injury, such as by falling or lifting something heavy. Chronic back pain is that which lasts more than three months and is often caused by a ruptured or bulging disc, arthritis, osteoporosis, scoliosis, or nerve pain. Some back pain is partly caused by inflammation, and numerous pre-clinical and animal studies have found benefits of CBD for inflammation. Through possible reductions in both nerve and inflammatory pain, CBD may help relieve back pain.

CBD LOTION FOR PAIN

When it comes to localized pain, topical CBD lotion or creams may be a great option. By applying the CBD directly to problem areas, concentrated CBD is delivered to exactly where you need it the most.

While human studies on the efficacy of CBD lotion are lacking, there are plenty of animal studies and personal accounts to support this use. Studies found that rats with arthritis treated with transdermal CBD experienced reductions in pain-related behaviors and inflammation.

DOSAGE AMOUNTS OF CANNABIS AND CBD FOR PAIN

Cannabis and CBD dosing for pain are highly individual. Studies have found a bell-shaped dose-response curve with cannabis extract, meaning that it slowly becomes more effective until it hits a certain point, and then the effectiveness decreases. To further complicate matters, the effective dose found in human studies varies greatly from one condition and one study to the next. For example, in migraines, the effective dose of THC and CBD was found to be 200 mg/day, with no benefits found at 100 mg/day. However, doses of Sativex, an oral spray that delivers 2.7 mg THC and 2.5 mg CBD per spray, was found to be effective in the treatment of central neuropathic pain in Multiple Sclerosis at doses of around 20-30 mg/day CBD + 22-32 mg/day THC.

CBD dosage for pain has not been examined in any human studies. Like the Cannabis sativa extract, studies have found that exceeding the optimal dose of CBD can lead to a reduction in efficacy. In a study examining the effect of CBD on anxiety, 100 mg and 900 mg were not effective, where 300 mg was. So where, then, should you start when it comes to dosing Cannabis sativa or CBD oil? Follow these steps when adding in a cannabis or CBD oil product:

1. Choose the product that you would like to take
2. Start at the lowest recommended dosage
3. Split this dose between 2-3 doses throughout the day
4. Stay at the same dose for 3 or more days, evaluating your response
5. Increase your dose until you find the best dose for you

CANNABIS SATIVA IS GOOD FOR PAIN

Studies and anecdotal reports have shown that cannabis is good for pain. Whether you enjoy smoking weed or not, there are numerous products available for you to use if you live in a state where pot is legal.

Some products that may help if you want something other than bud itself include:

- Lotions or creams

- Tinctures (dropper bottles with cannabis-infused oils)

- Capsules or pills

- Edibles (chocolates, candies, teas, or other foods infused with cannabis)

When looking at these products it is important to choose one that is a full-plant extract. This allows you to access the full potential of the wide array of healthful and anti-inflammatory compounds found in the Cannabis sativa plant.

SIDE EFFECTS

Most people tolerate CBD oil well, but there are some possible side effects.

The most common side effects include:
Fatigue

Diarrhea

Changes in appetite

Weight gain or weight loss

In addition, using CBD oil with other medications may make those medications more or less effective.

Also scientists are yet to study some aspects of CBD, such as its long-term effects on hormones. Further long-term studies will be helpful in determining any side effects CBD has on the body over time. Consult a doctor before using CBD, as it may interact with certain over-the-counter dietary supplements and medicines, as well as some prescription medications especially those that warn against consuming grapefruit. CBD might also interfere with an enzyme called cytochrome P450 complex. This disruption could affect the liver's ability to break down toxins, increasing the risk of liver toxicity. The patient information leaflet for Epidiolex cautions that there is a risk of liver damage, lethargy, and possibly depression and thoughts of suicide, but these potential side effects are true of other treatments for epilepsy, too. Study suggests cannabinoids' anti-inflammatory effect may reduce inflammation too much. A large reduction in inflammation could diminish the lungs' defense system, increasing the risk of infection.

OTHER CONSIDERATIONS

Almost all research on CBD oil and pain comes from adult trials. Experts do not recommend CBD oil for use in children, as there is little research on the effects of CBD oil on a child's developing brain.

However, people may use Epidiolex for children ages 2 and above who have rare forms of epilepsy. People should not use CBD oil when pregnant or breastfeeding. People should use caution when taking CBD products by mouth alongside high-fat meals. High-fat meals can dramatically increase the blood concentrations of CBD, which can increase the risk of side effects. The FDA does not regulate CBD products in the same way they regulate drugs or dietary supplements, so companies sometimes mislabel or misrepresent their products. That means it's especially important to do some research and find a quality product.

HOW LONG DOES CBD OIL TAKE TO WORK

To understand how long CBD takes to work, you first need a basic understanding of what CBD is, and how different variables can impact its onset of action. In general, CBD is absorbed into the bloodstream within 20 minutes to 2 hours depending on the method of delivery.1 Other variables like the dosage, full spectrum or THC-free, consistency, and quality can also play a role in how quickly you begin to feel the benefits of CBD. But there's one major caveat to all of this, it really depends on your goals and expectations. For those taking CBD for mild everyday stresses, you might find that your first dose gives you a relaxing effect that helps to manage your stress levels. However, for anyone trying CBD for a more serious issue, consistency and patience needs to be part of your wellness routine for the full potential of CBD to be realized.

HOW MUCH CBD SHOULD I TAKE?

The bottom line is that when you're choosing a CBD product, you should consider the type of ailment you're trying to treat and adjust your dosage accordingly. This may also include testing different consumption methods or a different application style. It can also depend on your body mass, and if you're taking any prescription medications. Everyone is different, and this is something you need to dial in for yourself. A full dropper of our 750 mg CBD oil is 25 mg, which we think is a great daily serving to start out. But some people take more, and some take less. You should also be careful to avoid self-medicating. CBD is a powerful supplement, especially when it contains THC alongside it. So it's best to consult with your doctor to determine the right dose for you and avoid any CBD side effects.

HOW LONG CBD TAKES TO ENTER YOUR BLOODSTREAM

As I mentioned above, the answer to how long CBD takes to work really depends on your own definition of the word "work." Taking CBD for mild anxiety is going to be much quicker and easier to treat than someone who is trying CBD for a more serious condition. Simply put, the answer to this question isn't a one-size-fits-all solution. It is a step by step approach that acknowledges how the benefits of CBD, and how long it takes to achieve them, may differ from different delivery methods and the issue at hand. For example: how long it takes CBD to work will differ drastically between sublingual oils, CBD capsules, and CBD topical.

FACTOR 1: METHOD OF INTAKE

There are many different ways to consume CBD. Each of these methods has a different impact on how much, and how quickly, the CBD gets absorbed into your bloodstream. This phenomenon is called bioavailability. It's important to understand this because it will help you determine how much you'll need to take to feel its effects; and you can also get an idea of how long it will take for your CBD to work.

The consumption method of CBD is the biggest determining factor in how long it may take for CBD oil to work. The quickest and most bioavailable method of CBD consumption is through inhalation. The next best is a sublingual oil or tincture, followed by ingestible CBD capsules and finally topicals. Because CBD capsules have to travel through your digestive system, they have what's known as a first-pass metabolism. This means that it'll take longer to feel the effects of the CBD, or in medical terms the bioavailability rate. (To clarify: this applies for all edible cannabis products, because all of them have to pass through your digestive system.) On the other hand, CBD oil avoids first-pass metabolism by going straight through the capillaries under your tongue. This makes it the most effective method of delivery to avoid smoking, and it means you'll feel it quicker. This is also the main reason we formulate our organic CBD oils with medium chain coconut oil. Because of its thin and viscous characteristics, it absorbs quickly when placed under the tongue. There are other variables at play in how long it takes, too; but this should help you determine when your specific form of CBD will start working.

FACTOR 2: DOSAGE & POTENCY

The amount of CBD you're taking every day will affect how quickly you will begin feeling its effects. In general, the more that you're taking, the quicker you'll feel it. For example, if you take a high dose of CBD to improve your sleep, you'll probably feel sleepy in about 15-30 minutes. In contrast, if you take a lower serving for general wellness, pain, or inflammation, it could take a few days of dosing to notice significant results.

FACTOR 3: CBD QUALITY

We've said it time and time again: not all CBD products are created equal. Because this market is largely unregulated, many brands on the market do very little to maintain the quality of their products. Some CBD brands use ingredients that have impurities, additives, and adulterants which will significantly affect the safety of your product. This is why you should always look for a third party lab test to know that you're getting a high quality CBD product. It is also recommended looking for a full spectrum product, which contains more cannabinoids than just CBD. Just like CBD, these other cannabinoids don't get you high; but they do have a synergetic effect that heightens your body's response. One of those cannabinoids is probably one you've heard a lot about, and that's THC. In order for a product to truly be considered full spectrum, make sure it contains trace amounts of THC. The legal amount is no more than 0.3% of total dry weight. The origin of the raw hemp plant material is another key factor that determines the quality of your product. Hemp is a powerful bioaccumulator, meaning that it soaks up all the nutrients and toxins in the soil it grows in. If the soil isn't pretested for toxins, pesticides, or heavy metals, those things could end up in your CBD.

In addition, if the farmer uses synthetic fertilizers, or if the field doesn't go through a multi-year crop rotation, there will be fewer nutrients in the soil and the hemp will contain less CBD. You can avoid all of these problems by opting for an organic cannabis product that's been certified by the USDA.

FACTOR 4: INDIVIDUAL BIOLOGY

Although you can count on certain effects to take place, no two people respond exactly the same to CBD, even if they have the same consumption, the same delivery method, and the same body composition. One person could feel their tincture in 10 minutes; yet someone else could take the same dose and feel it in an hour. There are several key considerations that fall into this category, and they all affect the amount of time it will take to feel CBD's effects.

FACTOR 5: CONSISTENCY

For some people, the positive effects come immediately. A lot of people will notice that they're experiencing less stress, less tension, and better sleep after just one dose of CBD. For others, though, it might take a few weeks to notice the powerful effects of CBD. So if you don't feel it right away, be patient. A lot of people give up after a few doses and brush it off as snake oil that doesn't work. This couldn't be further from the truth while these people might be taking a bad-quality product, they're also ignoring one of the key properties of CBD oil. Regardless of what you're feeling, the positive results come slowly. The key to getting the most benefits out of your CBD is consistency. A consistent, daily dose will eventually restore balance your ECS; and you'll be glad you stuck with it.

BODY WEIGHT

Like most cannabinoids, CBD is fat-soluble. Those who weigh more tend to have more fat cells in their body, which means that they'll absorb and store it for longer in their body. While this isn't necessarily a bad thing, it does mean that people with more fat cells in their body will most likely need more time to adjust. It's not all bad news, though: the higher your body mass, the longer it takes for CBD to work.

METABOLISM

While individual metabolism does involve burning calories, it also affects how your body breaks down compounds like CBD. Depending on your age, your lifestyle, your digestive system, and your genetic profile, your metabolism can function at different rates. This is what we call our metabolic rate and we all have different ones. If you exercise regularly and have a high metabolism, you'll feel the effects come on faster; but you'll also feel it wear off more quickly. On the other hand, if you have a slow metabolism, you'll notice that it takes longer to feel your CBD coming on; and it will stay in your body for longer.

ENDOCANNABINOID BALANCE

CBD is part of a unique set of compounds called cannabinoids. These compounds interact with a biological system found in nearly all mammals. It's called the endocannabinoid system (ECS), and its cannabinoid receptors are found throughout your entire nervous system. While we're just beginning to understand how the ECS works, research suggests that it's responsible for many of your biological functions like your mood, sleep, appetite, and pain response. If your ECS is imbalanced, you could experience a large range of negative symptoms as a result. CBD helps alleviate these symptoms by attaching to the receptors and rebalancing your endocannabinoid system. In general, the more your endocannabinoid system is imbalanced, the longer it will take to feel the effects. While there's no way to quantify how much of an imbalance you're experiencing; you can probably gauge this yourself by assessing the severity of your symptoms.

FEELING OUT HOW CBD WORKS FOR YOU

When you're new to CBD, the first thing to know is that the effects take a few days to become noticeable. That means when you begin taking CBD every day, it's good to be mindful of how your body responds to your daily CBD dosage. To discover its full effects, we recommend trying it for a full 30 days. Your first 30 days is an important time to better understand your body and how it responds.

The many therapeutic benefits that CBD oils and tinctures have to offer are becoming more recognized, making people interested in getting started. The first 30 days can be a trial and error time in finding what works best for the individual.

WHAT KIND OF CBD SHOULD I TAKE?

For first time users, it's advisable to start with full spectrum CBD oil, which you take sublingually which means a dropper of oil under your tongue for 30 to 60 seconds to let it absorb through the mucus membrane in your mouth. Some people have trouble taking CBD hemp oil under the tongue, and so they prefer the CBD capsules. They are also worth considering if you're experiencing inflammation in the lower digestive tract, as the capsules get further down into the gut. People looking for pain relief in a specific area often use a CBD lotion on the affected area, almost anywhere on the human body (avoid the eyes and mucus membranes to avoid irritation). For best results, pairing CBD lotion with sublingual oil, and using the same delivery methods at the same time every day.

You'll also always want to make sure whatever CBD product you are using has third party lab tests. The best companies have a QR code, and all of their company information, and testing lab information readily available to be reviewed before or after purchase. In order for CBD oil to work, you must first make sure that what you're taking is real! If you can't view the third party test results before making your purchase, then hold off till you can do the research. Unfortunately, many unscrupulous vendors sell fake CBD oil. This is actually just hemp seed oil with a fake concentration listed on the bottle. You'll also want to stay away from any vendor that is making lofty health claims as CBD oil, and any cannabis extract for that matter, has not yet been approved by the FDA.15

WHAT TIME OF DAY SHOULD I TAKE IT?

This answer is different for everyone. The important thing is to find a time of day to best incorporate CBD into your daily routine. If you're suffering from discomfort and inflammation during the day, maybe it's best to take it in the morning. But if you're using CBD because you've read reports that it can help you sleep, then taking it just before bedtime is your sweet spot.

HOW OFTEN SHOULD I TAKE CBD?

To begin, start taking CBD once per day, a full dropper of 25 milligrams, or 50 milligrams if you're using our new extra strength CBD oils. See how you're feeling and sleeping. For first time users, it can be good to "load dose" at first taking larger than normal servings. That means, take a full dropper in the morning, and another full dropper before bedtime. You have taken too much if you feel groggy in the morning, or if you experience diarrhea symptoms. If you feel these side effects, dial back your current daily dosage to find something that works best for you. How often you take CBD may also play a role in a drug test or work related drug screenings. After taking it consistently for a period of weeks, the cannabinoids begin to build up within our systems, especially in body fat cells, which could cause you to test positive on lab tests during drug screenings. If drug testing is a concern for your job, talk to your HR department before you start taking it consistently. You may also consider switching to a CBD topical.

HOW LONG DOES IT TAKE FOR CBD TO WORK?

It takes a few days, and it's not something that you'll notice right away. Be mindful of any pain, anxiety, and sleep patterns as you work through your first week. Keep journal entries to track sleep and progress, and the amount of CBD you're taking. This will help you be aware of the effects of CBD on your body. Understand that health benefits from natural supplements like CBD edibles, CBD tincture and oils don't happen overnight. It takes time for the human body to adjust after implementing several different changes into our lifestyle. It also depends on the amount of CBD you're taking to really experience the true effects of CBD products.

CONCLUSION

While many studies have suggested CBD oil is helpful for pain, more research is necessary, especially long-term studies with human subjects. However, CBD oil does show promise as a treatment for pain. Some scientific and anecdotal evidence suggests that it can help people manage chronic pain in various contexts. CBD oil is especially promising due to its lack of intoxicating effects and a possible lower potential for side effects than many other pain medications. People should discuss CBD oil with their doctor if they are considering using it for the first time.

Made in United States
Orlando, FL
10 March 2023

30900215R00033